I0426626

Époque

by

The Artist

This book is a work of fiction. Places, events, and situations in this story are purely fictional. Any resemblance to actual persons, living or dead, is coincidental.

© 2004 by The Artist. All rights reserved.

No part of this book may be reproduced, stored in a retrieval system, or transmitted by any means, electronic, mechanical, photocopying, recording, or otherwise, without written permission from the author.

First published by AuthorHouse 05/12/04

ISBN: 1-4184-7197-6 (e-book)
ISBN: 1-4184-2579-6 (Paperback)

This book is printed on acid free paper.

Dedication

This book is dedicated to my mother Danielle and Marsha my sister who always said gently with her words that your talent will take you far in life if you believe in yourself, thanks to you both for making me realizing how of a wonderful being I am. This book is also dedicated to a very special man who help me to be that special person in society's eyes, God without your true words I know my soul would be lost. "Here's to you Lord for blessing me daily".

Special Thanks

William Coss thank you for going out of your way to help me reach certain goals in my life, without your boost I would of giving up, but it is you who saw the sparkling light in me and allowed me to shine. In advance, thank you for taking the time of day to discover the magic that lies in me.

About The Author

Growing up in the island was hard for many middle class families unless you had inherited your parent's trust funds at that time. I never understood what I went through growing up, but the only thing that matters to me was being inspired by poetry. Later on when I became a little bit older to understand the meaning behind certain poems, it is then I discover my passion for writing poetry. I guess it was away for me to ease my pain for not being love enough or consolidate the drama in my life, such as falling in love with the wrong people. As an adult I began to search for answers but to find God as my witness and of course my poems for guidance

Table of Contents

First Love 1

Fear 2

Relationship 3

The Lover 4

True Love 5

Lost Soul 6

Confession 7

Jeunne Homme 8

Freedom 9

Just Making It 10

Old Love 11

Fortune Teller 12

The Last Word 13

Some Say Love 14

J'ai Perdue Mon Chemin 15

Hope 16

Here I Shall Wait' 17

Slaves 18

Unheard Prayer 19

Open Eyes 20

Silken Cloth 21

No More Pain 22

Heart Breaker 23

Ungrateful Path 24

The Path To Holiness 25

The Voice 26

Forgiveness! 27

11/11/2002 29

The Hurt! 30

Thank You Alexander Santiago! 31

Alexander's Pride 32

The Miracle of you! 33

Magic Moments! 34

The Lesson 35

Try Again 36

Mother's Strength 37

Mother's Pain 38

June 16th 2001 39

Soul Mate 41

Sinners 42

Last Spoken Word 43

The fire within 44

Rage 45

Forever His 46

He Is, I am 47

Invisible You Think! 48

Goals 51

Trademark 52

Unbreakable! 53

First Love

I have learned not to worry about love;
But to honor its coming with all my
heart.
I ne'er was struck before that hour
with love so sudden and sweet, her
face it bloomed like a sweet flower
and stole my heart away complete.

To examine the dark mysteries of the
blood with headless heed and swirl,
to know the rush of feelings swift and flowing
as water. She seemed to hear my silent voice,
not love's appear to know.

I have learned not to worry about love;
but to honor its worth with all my heart.

Fear

Oh Father I am coming, please open your arms.
for I know there is a reason to be "very"
much alarmed.
It is a voice I hear. He has called to me.
Oh Father I am scared, this voice I hear
is not righteous you see.
The Beast he is coming, I can feel he is near.
Oh Father save my soul, for tomorrow
you promised us eternal life.
Oh Father I stand before you, is it too late?
Oh Father, out of his mouth, the Beast speaks
my name. But I wish not to be the one burn
in his flame.
Oh Father protect me from unrighteousness and Evil.
Oh Father I have spoken, please tell me you hear.

Relationship

I loved you; even now my tongue may confess,
I love your lips when they're wet with wine
and red with a wild desire.

Give all to love; obey thy heart:
Knows its path, and the outlets of the sky-so kiss
me sweet with your warm wet mouth, still
the joys of a living love.

I loved you for what you are, but I love you
not so much for your realities as for your ideas
I pray for your desires that they may be great,
rather than for your satisfaction, which may
be hazardous to your health.

Do not follow it utterly, but hope beyond hope
that this love may last for eternity

The Lover

I cannot swear with certainty that I will feel as I do now,
nor can I promise stars forever bright.
I cannot see beyond this present night to say
what promises the dawn may hold.

I love you now for the part of me you bring out,
not so much for the person you aren't-but for the
love you can offer me.
The love I bear for thee is pure and everlasting,
finding words enough, and hold the torch out
while the winds are enough.

Obey thy heart; plans, give all to love, let it have
scope, hope beyond hope; high and more high
with wing unspent. Untold intent, but it's God
who knows our true intentions, knows our path,
and the outlets of the sky.

True Love

My true love hath my heart, and I have his, by just
exchange one for another given.
All my past life is mine no more;
The flying hour are gone, whose image I kept in store
by memory alone.

Love you sweet, with all my heart, feeling, thinking,
seeing;
Love you in the lightest part, love you in full being.
Love you with open arms in its frank surrender,
love you with my thinking soul, break it to love
sighing, my true love is near.

Stay, O sweet, and do not rise, the light that shines comes
from thine eyes;
The day breaks not, it is my heart, stay, or else my joys
will die, and perish in their infancy.

Lost Soul

I will weave great melodies for my soul,
I will seek me a way no man has trod,
I will blaze new trails to the heart of God-
that my soul may walk wider ways than earth,
my soul and the souls of the world.

I will hew great spaces for my soul, to know what
the void life may reveal. That the claims of the
earth may not bind me, that death may not find me,
that my passionate spirit have room to grow,
that the sadness of the earth may not 'numb me and
grief overcome me.

I will capture the chords of thundering years, that my
spirits pain may cease. That my eyes may meet God's
eyes and know, I will hew great window's, wonderful
windows, measureless windows, for my soul.

Confession

Though I speak with the tongue of men and of
angles, and have not charity, I have become a
dreamer.
Tonight I close my eyes and feel the silent,
I am become as the sounding brass,
or a thinking symbol to thy heart.

We are not lovers, we have lived and loved
together, I cry your mercy-pity-me not, for
I grieve and do not show my discontent.

I love my lady; she is very fair; as bliss of saints,
when dreaming of large wings, the bloom around
her fancied presence flings, her spirit sits aloof,
and high, sweetly and tenderly.

I love you for your brownness, and the rounded brightness
of your breast, I love you for the breaking gladness in your voice-
A perfect woman, nobly planned, and now I see.

Jeunne Homme

I am black, a young black man, and once I laughed in boyish glee;
For one of my colour stood in the track where drivers drove,
and looked at me pass, and from that hour my spirits grew as free
as if unsold, unbought;
I am black; I am black, a young black man, and black am proud.

Freedom

"Make way for liberty!" he cried;
Made way for liberty, and die!
It must not be; this day, this hour,
and now the work of life and hung
on the passing of a breath;

Yet, while freedom depend on one,
Indeed: Behold at last!
The sounds wave across the nations ears.

Freedom we seek, for every freeman was a host,
for every hour we counted, they come to conquer
or to fall, how could they rest within graves,
and leave their homes the homes of slaves.

Just Making It

I stood among the wanting many my heart was heavy,
for its trust had been abused, its kindness answered with
foul wrong;

If the faults or the crimes of thy youth are a burden too heavy to bear,
what hope can re-bloom on the desolate waste of a jealous despair?
I know how the spirit hearkens to voices of doubt or of doom;

I know how the tempter mutters the terrible word, "despair!"
Let others sing to the hero who wins in the ceaseless fray,
oh God I know how the gray cloud darkens, and mantles the soul in gloom;
no failure was recorded, but victory accepted in the eyes of many.

Old Love

You have come to the end of the highway, traveler, here where the last relationship
waits;
You have come to the end of the long road, traveler, here where the heart grew pale.

And there's never a chance it's the wrong road, traveler,
winding beyond the vale;
You have turned at last from the byway, traveler,
In through the twilight gates;

Once when your heart was passion-free to learn of things divine,
the soul of nature suddenly outpoured itself in mine.

To one in all, to all in one, I hold the secrets of the deep,
and the heavens above;
Come along, true believer, come along!
De way is open wide:

I hold the secrets, I have my own ambition. It is not to mount or confuse you- but to
reveal the passion and the mysteries of love.

Fortune Teller

The world, you advise me, is utterly wrong,
my life, you assure me, is sad;
that luck is against you, my friend, you can see
you have reason, to believe, but why must you tell
all your troubles to me—when I'm dying to tell mine to you!

The Last Word

I will soar on symphonies of might, lifted and carried that earth may hear—
and rejoice;
I will summon the stars for their voice, I will summon the suns.
I will mount and mount on wings of sound,
I will challenge the void where secrets of life are furled,
I will cleave new paths, that all may have fresh birth.

Some Say Love

Some say love is a myth, and some say it's a miracle,
some say it makes the world go around, some say
that love is troublesome.

If all the world and love were young, and truth in every
shepherd's tongue, these pretty pleasures might me move
like the Hudson River Stream.

And when I asked the woman next-door, who looked as if
she knew, all I got was a quite tone;
where true love burns desire is Love's pure flame,
It is the reflex of our earthly frame that takes its meaning
from the nobler part, and but translate the language of the heart.

J'ai Perdue Mon Chemin

The hope I dreamed of was a dream, was but a dream; and now I wake,
I turn aside, I turn about, I fight the battle in my heart 'cause' I'm lost.

I walk by day, I walk by night, thirsting, panting for your face–
and ever, ever were you to be found.

I turn aside, I turn about, and still love beckons, burning bright–
and ever, ever facing me;
I fight the battle in my heart, and wavering is the victory;
and I pray to God for strength, I wonder if God hears my prayers,
and–may he now forgive the thought– I sometimes wonder if God cares.

Hope

I am a young man, full of strength and hope,
I am a hard worker sold to the 9 to 5 work.

O, let me be a man again- and dream,
I am the people, worried, hungry,
I am the man beaten, I am the man who never
got ahead, the poorest worker bartered through the years.

Sure, call me a lazy worker, for I'm the one who left my
country to seek many opportunities.

I am the immigrant clutching the hope I seek-
I am the Negro bearing slavery's scars.
I am the red man driven from the land, and finding only
the same old stupid plan of dog eating dog, and the weak becomes weaker.

I am the man who dreamt a dream so strong, so brave, so true,
that even yet it's mighty daring sings- and yet I swear this oath,
I am the man who finally got ahead despite the jealousy of others.

I am the man who fought for freedom of the spirit, which takes you to higher
ground- I am the same colored man you kicked, fought and disrespected
I am a man of many colors what the eyes can see on the outer skin-
I am a man who believes in freedom despite the color of the skin.

Here I Shall Wait'

Here I shall wait to meet the rush of some relentless fate,
here I shall stand against misfortune, with its crushing hand,
and, though I fear I shall see starlight in the sky, yet I should
struggle upward, bit by bit, until my soul fight for more
important goal.

Say "I will!" and then stick to it- that's the only way to do it.

Here I shall stand against the bitter sword, that life may wave;
where I will hold to one eternal dream of valor riding roughshod to the grave.

Slaves

I've come this far to freedom and I won't turn back.
I've found my destination and I've made my vow;
I've prayed and slaved and waited and I've sing my song.

Courage!-nothing e'er withstood freemen fighting for their good;
Courage!-freedom I shouted, who will be a slave? Freemen shouted
again, and again, free 'em before the sunset pass, like the thief of the
night.

Courage!-I've seen the daylight breaking through the mighty valley
loom before me and I won't stop now- till the day I'm free.

Unheard Prayer

Long they have beat with timid hands upon life's leaden door,
praying the patient, yet remain the close, unheeded and unheard,
they have dreamed as young men dream of glory, love and power;

They have hoped as youth will hope of life's sun-minted hour.
The strong demand, contend, prevail;
They have seen as others saw, and they have learned to live it down
as though did not care.

Open Eyes

Here's to your eyes for the things I see
my little stone sinks quickly into the bosom of this deed,
dark River of oblivion......

here's to your body I desire
may it ever be full of the love of loving....

Here's to your heart for the things I see
may you never be drowned?
Here's to your lips I kissed two livid streaks of flame....

Here's to your soul, may it have eternal life in the eyes
of the people who care,
here's to our love I've cherished
may it grow to a higher level...

Silken Cloth

I wished, as I viewed my dreams in a silken cloth, and laid them away in a box of gold;

I wished, as I viewed my life in a silken cloth, and laid them away in a box of gold;

I have wrapped my dreams and love in a silken cloth, and laid Them away in a box of gold;

I hide no hate; I am not even wroth
I wished, as I fear death and laid it away in a box of gold-and feel no pity to what the earths bring.

I play it cool and dig all jive. That's the reason I stay alive, so that I can love and laid them in a box of gold.

No More Pain

Now you will feel no pain,
for you will be shelter with the kindness of my heart.

Now you will feel no sadness,
for you will have my warmth daily.

Now you will feel no more loneliness,
for you will be companion by me.

Now we are two bodies,
seeking each other sweet caress.

I am the way you seek,
and therefore I challenge you.

Heart Breaker

Now you will feel no pain, for you will be sheltered
I loved you with all my will, but much against my heart,
we two now part.
I do not want to sadden you again-for I am a heart breaker
all my past life is mine no more;
whatever is to come is not: The flying hour is gone,
my love fleeting away like Duck's fleeting south for the winter.

If I, by miracle, can be this lifelong love true to thee, let us use it while we may
let us not take this love for granted, or snatch those joys that haste away!

Whatever is to come is not: For still the charmer I approve, in hours of bliss
we oft have met; and though the present I cannot bear, I'm grateful for the past.

Ungrateful Path

I walk the path of ungratefulness without looking back at my past-
or what to expect for the future
I walk the path of unfaithfulness without understanding the hurt I
cause many alone my way
I walk the path of so many like the wind I lift-up so many souls
I walk the path and saw my journey through like a dead soul without cause
I pour out my soul to reach out to those I left behind, realizing I must continue
I walk the path once more there the answer awaits me the further I go
I walk and realized my mission is incomplete
I walk the path with my head high without anyone pulling me down
I walk the path skillfully knowing there I will be recognized someday.

The Path To Holiness

Never mind a change of scene–try a change of thinking.
Rise! For the day is passing. The path he choose is clear
rise! For he is risen and behold the truth!
let others sing to thee for he is Holy!
let not the soul to perish but to have wisdom of the Lord
If an unkind word appears while your journey adjourned–
let not the ear to listen; If suspicion come to you that your
journey isn't safe trust in the word of Holiness.
let the long contention cease! When earth seems dark with envy
and hate or greed distract you call onto thee for courage!

Rise for he is risen and behold the truth!
Rise for the day, the hour is passing the path you choose is clear
if some bit of gossip occurs, trust in thee for understanding
if unkind word appears try to listen with a clear mind
do this for a little while, then go out and burn the file.

The Voice

If I knew you and you knew me- if both of us could clearly see or hear,
the voice so clear, so powerful, so inviting, only the inner sight divine
the meaning of your heart in mine, I'm sure that we would change many minds
our thoughts would pleasantly agree if I knew you and you knew me.

The world is exceedingly large and problems are very complex;
we must have faith in ourselves, and we have faith in thee when trouble appears;
though all questions have two sides at least, it is thyself alone that may thyself betray.

If I knew you and you knew me, we could look at each other in the face for comfort-
I'm sure that we would give more and see therein the voice truer grace.
Just to be tender, just to be true the voice you hear is mighty-
Follow it utterly and let it guide you to a place only peace is the key to your salvation.

Forgiveness!

My heart was heavy for many days, for its trust had been broken and been abused
my spirit wrongfully crushed with the hand of someone I love-finding the mystery
of an old flame recapture in the spur of the moment, my joy was simply pushed aside
to bitterness;

Yes! The heart of man, walk in which way it will, not realizing the hurt of many or the soul
It destroys. Hope of all passion, most of mine came from thy heart, joy and tears I shed
not knowing where to go for I love this man strongly.

Yes! My heart was heavy for many nights, for its trust had been abused, its kindness answered
to the mistakes I've yet to forgive-do I remain confine there with tears?
I will soar here where the terror affected me the most, I will cleave new paths, that all may
seek new direction, I will breathe new air and that the being of me have room to grow, that my
eyes may be open to new possibilities.

Yes! If I endure I must go on enduring and my reward for pain –is pain;
Yet, though the hope, the thrill, the trust I once had for this man may take awhile to come back-
In my heart I fear not the manipulator driven him to such act, but to forgive him with all my
heart and keep our love growing.

It takes great strength to bring your life up square after knowing you've been emotionally
destroyed by the one love you trusted; It takes courage to finally come to a conclusion you will
forget and simply take that to the next level. Shit dangerous risk I'm willing to take without the
acceptance of my friends or my family to back me up, knowing when the shit fall it falls hard
enough to bring me back to those empty nights I sadden myself to sleep.

It takes great strength to live where I belong with the one I love,

The Artist

when other people think that I'm wrong for taking a chance, people you love, approval is a
pleasure you choose;
In living my belief- well, it takes strength, and courage, too.

11/11/2002

I'm sorry," said Hillis, "but I don't know what got to me.
This are the sins I fain, without realizing the pain I cause
but at last I've learned an important lesson to let go of Ryan;

I want him to know how much pain he let me endure while feelings
of an old boyfriend came back to mind, but only to see his weakness taking-
control over his mind and body.

I have been a little used and betrayed by the only thing my heart seeks-
yet, I say these words so that he can hear and feel my pain,
you hurt me, why? Where everywhere I looked Ryan's name popping as a reminder-
to remind me of that terrible night I wish not to recall, but every time I look there
he is the unfavorable, vicious man who had stolen my pure and most precious gold.

The Hurt!

Life has hurt to sell- all the impossible and splendid things,
If this little world tonight can be mine I would seek me a new way,
If this splendid world can be mine, only then my spirit will sign the cost for peace.

Worry stalked me along the way, trouble sneaking after me;
Friends becoming my enemies, and grief taking over my spirit for those I lost-
Father I have loved-but I have lost- I have fought- but I have failed;
I have paid bitter cost, yet my heart never quailed;
I have fallen, yet I rise to face my destiny- and today I stand tall to fight back.

Thank You Alexander Santiago!

I am tired of fighting for love and realizing all I get back is a slap in the face
I am sick of showy seeming of life that is half a lie, of faces that reminds me
of mistakes I left unsolved.
I can feel no pride, but pity, for the burdens I left you behind to endure;
Yes, you felt at that daring hour, the night we met and made love like two birds in love,
you held my hand as I shifted gear, hoping this love will last, but only to find bitterness
ahead

No! I can feel no pride, but pity, for the trouble I put you through;
There is nothing sweet facing the world alone with thoughts in mind unfulfilled-
looking back
I can only say, thank you for loving me for the short time we shared I know it hasn't
been easy.

Thank you for the hurt you've also cause me, but now my eyes are open to many things
thank you for being evil the way you were without doubts you were hurting me
thank you at the end for supporting me when times were hard, and I will never forget
that
thank you for moving me away no one has ever moved me, and I thank God for the end.

Alexander's Pride

I could say nice things about him;
I could thank him if I would;
I could tell the world about him
and his right doing by me, all I recall the memory I refuse to escape me.

I could speak wonder about him, a man every man hearts desires
I could let the entire world know I appreciate his kindness
that he's often shown to me, and it will not be forgotten~
I could boost him as he journeys out there in NYC looking for a new~ for I'm one of
those now waiting patiently for his forgiveness, and I've
not say a word;
I seek his face to thank him for opening my eyes, and only finding hate
I could continue to search for his presence~but at the present his pre-
occupy with another. As a man it's good to know I have not failed;
and perhaps someday Alex will set aside his pride and finally face me.

The Miracle of you!

Quietly you came into my life
Openly you shared your life with me
Gently you made a difference in my life
Tenderly you touched my soul
Gratefully I celebrate the beauty of each moment
Shared with you
Thank you for the miracle of you....
You are, and always will be, the love of my life.

Magic Moments!

I remember vividly the last time I cried
I alter my perception of my life my self esteem at that point was knock
down until there's was you.
Being apart from you isn't easy. I find myself missing you so often,
in so many ways.
Falling in love with you is the best thing that's ever happened to me.
with your sense of humor, your caring way, and your understanding, you
taught me to believe.
Nothing in this world has ever meant so much to me as the love we're in
now.
And I know that I could never love anyone else the way that I love you.
But even though I find myself missing you so often, gentle thoughts of you fill my
days, and dreams of you fill my nights.

The Lesson

It's easy to smile and be cheerful when everything's pleasant and fair;
A laugh is just like sunshine, that freshens all the day, when there are no burdens to bear.
So much to do: so little done! Never give up! It is wiser and better yet always to hope, than one to despair;
The day has been vague, and my heart has been black, cries humor, fear, hope and worries over come me.

No man, however good, but many try, many failed
the lesson I've learned had made me stronger than life itself~I smile awhile there is always
room for advance, but the road that leads me to you had taught me a lesson to be strong
I appreciate the kindness that life has to offer me, but yet there's still a lesson to be learn.

Try Again

It is a lesson you should fear, try, and try again;
If at first you don't succeed, try, and try again;
If you find your task is hard, time will bring your reward, try, and try again;
For, if you will persevere, you will conquer, never fear; try, and try again.

If you have a friend worth loving, love him! And let him know this that you love
him, if you hear a song that make you sad, try, and try again.
If your heart aches for the right one, try to overcome the pain
If you see the hot tears falling from your lover's weeping eyes, share them!

Once or twice though you should fail, pick up yourself and try again;
It is a lesson you should heed, try, and try again;
Why, with patience, should not you?
Only keep this in mind the lesson learned: do this and you should succeed.

Mother's Strength

Mother your strength has taught me to be the man I am today
without you my soul would be lost, or perhaps never be;
You say keep your head up high when life is hard and never give up
no matter what the circumstances are, remember where you came from.

My mother's strength and beliefs help me to overcome my fear when I had doubts
she taught me to believe in myself enough to know right from wrong, regardless what
Others had to say badly about me.
Mother with your vision and the pain you endure, and pain you faced, made you the
unbreakable woman that you are I am proudly to say I love you.

I remember at times when I felt like giving up, even though you're not around your
voice I can hear start to echo in the room just to remind me you will guide me- no
matter what.   You said with a solid tone to be strong never to give up: do I remain
silent waiting for you to make your move!
Yes, my mother's strength and hope that she has in God never fails but always
prevail even when times are hard, she always bounce back to victory.

My mother battle for a very long time with her faith in God and even questioned it at
the end she never, ever worry cause she knows the Lord have something good in
store for her. I often never seen my mother cry, her face as she looked at me and
said my children are my strength and I would do anything to see that they're happy.

Mother's Pain

I often pray that my mother would find a companion in this world
someone who can make her feel like a princess, someone who's love so pure so strong
her weaknesses would appear.
Often I pray for this to happen never a miracle come about, only to start where I left off
her pain and loneliness we faced together hoping her Prince would come to her rescue
she sat there quietly patiently waiting hoping a moment of truth soon to come.
My mother's pain is more tense than it appears to be, her fear of losing her children
become silent in her heart.
I began to cry to see how hard my mother's life been in the past and continuously, do I
have the power to change it, say I do this, how can I make it a better place for her.

June 16th 2001

You came like the dawn with a voice slowly walked pass me in the hot summer day
You walked and smiled, looking back at me as if you can touch my soul without a doubt
I say it plain, and remembered perfectly the place on 47th street between the avenues, as you pass
me by, looking back wishing I'll be the one to deliver you from that terrible year of your 25th
birthday.
O, yes I would never forget the outfit, the cap with the letter 'H' you wore that day; as you
slowly took the time of day as my scent carried away and gave you a slap in the face;
If I had the time to find a place I would go back to the first moment I laid eyes on you
If I had the time to let my heart speak out and take in my life a part, to look about and stretch a
hand as you looked into my eyes that very evening as you entered Duane Read- only then I
would comfort you from the pain you endure.

There are roads in life that lead us through rough times and give us guarantees
Tomorrow, ah, tomorrow, we may think of life as something that is built up from a dream;
We may fall awaken from the trance of loving someone who's heart is cold, colder than ice;
We may hear an old song that call us, where memoirs are set aside;
and though hearts and hope are breaking as we come to bitter waking, yet the only road worth
taking is the road that leads us uphill.

I heard your voice crying out for a soul mate, searching for that true love without fear
Into all lives some rain must fall, into all eyes some tear-drops start,
whether they fall as gentle shower, or fall like fire from an aching heart left alone in your hotel
room that night, above all I felt your sincerity.
You came like the dawn with no voice, with a voice and a solution to your prayer I came to
claim you from the lost and found, and now with all my heart I plan on giving you
the fairy tale that your heart seeks.

Here, like a stranger stranded in the north, looking for love hoping you will speak

The Artist

as you pass me, all I got was a picture of that smile that led me to search for you on the number

one, nine train going to the upper west side of Manhattan, struggling to see your sweet face- but

never finding you. Yes, the search continues for I remain calm hoping some day you'll show up,

and then finally that day came there you have it love for eternity.

Soul Mate

I cannot see beyond this present night on my birthday to say
what promises you may hold in your heart, as I lie there with
a high fever and you taking the time to take care of me my heart
slowly beat with a cause, hoping you are the truth.

With all my will, but much against my heart, I fight this battle
a battle to an open heart, searching for the unforgettable; Yes,
call me crazy for I am near thee, my heart in the distance beats
close to thy heart.
I sleep with thee, and wake with thee, and yet I still to learn thee;
I fill my arms with thoughts of thee, that is, my soul mate, and press
the common air.
I think and speak of thee to keep my mind at rest, but still to thee
my memory clings like love in man's chest.

Oh I have sown my love so wide to thee that he will find it everywhere;
It will awake him in the night, it will enfold him in the air.
and I have winged it with desire, that it may be a cloud by day and in the night
a shaft of fire that's unfold like a fire dragon.
I think and speak of my soul mate and beyond this moment his eyes will open
I think and speak of him no matter where that his legacy and passion will ease me
Yes, the love I have for this man not only sustain me, but gives me courage.

Sinners

O foolish me Lord I have sin without regrets for your forgiveness
the secret of the Lord is with those who fear him, and he will show
them his covenant.
O foolish me Lord I have sin again and again, without fear of your wrath
I show no mercy to those I choose to hurt nor do I care to listen to their cries
I plead not, for I have no mercy to the souls I tear apart;
O foolish me Lord I have forsaken those who walk in my path, and I let them burn
I show them the way to hell like a sinner would do without any sympathy, O Lord
my soul is lost for I am a sinner with to much desire to what the earth hold
I began to weep, hoping you will come to my rescue, realizing you had forsaken me.

Last Spoken Word

Hear me Lord for my need have not been met
listen to my cries when I'm filled with doubts
deliver me from evil for I sit with the evildoers
choose not only the strong minded but also the weak
Guide me not into temptation but deliver me from evil
how lovely is your tabernacle, O Lord of host!
Purity you are, lost I am, deliver me
Purify my spirit and my tongue to speak righteously
Listen to my cries, O Lord of host for this is my last spoken word.

The fire within

I can feel the fire burning deep inside like a dragon in rage
no where to run but trying to escape insanity, the mortals
had discovered my secret but wanting to share it with the rest of the world
and use that against me in order to destroy my kind.
Yes, indeed I speak of history! I fought a good fight by their side to save human kind
but only to see this day will come, when one of them would betray me.

While the voice of the world shouts its chorus, my people were murdered
while the trumpet is sounding, many of my people were put to death–
with death sweeping down, countries being claimed, I watch the mortal faces

True I can feel the fire burning deep inside, but at that time all I can think of is to
destroy the mortals as they destroyed my people;
why must I feel pity for them while they're glad to destroy my kingdom, and stole
the young generation of my people for experiment.

I come not hear to talk. I come simply to redeem peace among my people and the
mortals who once believe my power will save them to salvation;
truly I can relate to their fears perhaps someday my people will turn and use their
powers like mutant against them but I cannot understand after all these years I
would have to choose, their lives, or the lives of my people.

Rage

Rage of a black panther is how I view myself
many can say I have a temper of a dragon or a black panther,
when I'm emotionally taking advantage of
Rage I cannot allowed anyone else to experience with me, nor can I
allow my friends to for see the evil that lies within

Rage is cause out of anger-rage is emotions
Rage is simple,
loosing control,
being hurt emotionally,
have no one to turn to,
feeling betrayed,
finding your love one cheating,
lack of sex,
lack of spiritual guidance,
Rage is......

Forever His

Fast this life of mine was dying, blind already and calm as death,
love came by, and having known him in a dream that would never end,
my heart grew heavier for this love, I've seen him only in a dream, but have not yet
to experience so far, and knowing this dream of mine someday will come true.
love bade him welcome; yet his face seemed puzzled like can this be for real-
the closer he gets to know me forever his I remain.

He Is, I am

He cannot be certain that he will feel the same way for the next 10 years
must I, what shall I do?-I'll sit me down simply to think, then I'll let him
know my true intentions.
let me be brave! For he is what I am and the more I see him the more my heart desire
him
wow! Love is so pure and wonderful between us and knowing what I know when I
looked
Into his eyes my heart is at peace.
He is, I am, the love of his life forever.

Invisible You Think!

Though I thought I was prepared, Hillis news shocked me. I knew in my heart
his health was a big question mark but that did not stop me to see his inner beauty-
people think it is wrong to love someone when they've been affected. My heart should be
used to this, my heart does not stop for death but it hurts. It was his faith that brought
us
together and death that will pull us apart.

"Did it surprise me when he told me his big secret?" I figured all alone I waited for
this love
for so long to just let secrets divide us apart, in fact I've waited 2 years to be by his side
and knowing what I know I sustained him when his most vulnerable.

Just as he is, my arms were opened to the truth but knowing the truth now makes me love
him
I'm lucky that he has giving me a choice to choose and was quite honest exposing the
truth no
matter what my decision would be now that is a person who is not invisible facing
reality.

I use to think I was invisible after taking this vow to be with this man regardless if his
infected- at first it strike me as a bad dream I'm not ready to face, but when I awake it
would go
away, Instead my heart felt heavy if I back out now knowing the vow I already took
when he
proposed for better or for worst till death to us apart and that is to be taking seriously.

All that I know of a certain person, is, it can never be simple when love is right and in
life's
noisiest hour, the presence of love is greater than anything, than it stops like a bird; like a
flower, blooming in the spring.   What matters to me is to see that love overcome us and
allow
us to be free.   How beautiful, how beautiful it seemed when two people believed in
serendipity or faith that can only be found within-Yes I began to shiver down my spine
knowing if exposing myself than I would be risking my own health to.

Invisible I used to believe I am but after meeting this man I knew than my life would
change

forever. "I know home is where my heart is but damn that! I wanna be where the rest of him is

at." A solitude moment I experience sustains the bed on which we lie, my dear Hillis.

Dear Hillis,

Well, my love, sometimes shit happens when you least expect it. I guess the fact that you're reading this letter means that I'm strong enough to fight with you till the end. That is unless I screwed things up. I know I ask you for a lot of favors and you've always delivered.

I have to say you are a very special person and I will always love you no matter if I'm gone before you, my presence will always be here to see you through. I'm writing because words are tough these days and I want to thank you for being the best friend a lover can have.

The last two months, though filled with great emotional pain, have been among the best in my life. Spending my days looking into your beautiful eyes and seeing the warmth and love sparkling like tiny diamonds against a black velvet sky.

It is worth waking up to you every day. I know I've giving you a hard time about the incident that happened between you in Ryan but now I forgive you in order to move on emotionally.

You know one of the truly sad things about your illness is facing it alone and not able to go out in reach youngster like yourself the cost of prevention.

There were times I sat in front of the computer thinking of all the good you and I can do in this world but in reality money is stopping us from achieving that particular goal. You know so many people go through life without ever knowing true friendship- or true love. We spend our lives trying to find someone to love us, or to love what we want them to think we are. But true friends accept you for you and that my friend is a joy. A joy I would have never known had I not met you. Hillis the two hardest things you are is black and a black gay man in which in this world is hard to face. Now back to you, I want you to live your life the way you feel most comfortable. Please know that Christ made you from his own image. If it's good enough for him why worry about mere mortals.

Cherish the friendship you have with me and with your aunt and with your mom knowing we will all be there for you when times are hard. Thank you, my sweet prince, for the friendship, the love, and giving my life so much meaning, memories, and magic. Now do not cry any sad tears get back to life, it's not over Hillis, you can only cry happy tears for you shall always remember my love for you is greater than anything in this world.

Love always,
Sunshine

Goals

Three summers have gone since the first time I had this dream, and still in vain I know not
what harbor I seek; if a man knows not what harbor he seeks, no light will guide him-
through this journey I became alert, joyful with no sadness for the presence of God is
with me.

We don't see things as they are, we see things as we are and that lead us to temptation;
Understanding our goals and dreams we can make a difference.
It is hard at times being the follower when indeed you're a leader, life need not
interruptions, in fact
desire deceived us.

Don't tell the world that you're waiting for me you know the world can be my biggest
enemy.
I'll sing and laugh at thy neglect, but never let it be constant in my favor, I'll serve my
purpose
In such noble ways was never heard before;
Ah! How oft have I whispered, how oft have I try to reply to those neglect, and
breathed my soul's
Question of "when shall it be?"

You know a good leader must also be a good follower in order to succeed, how long and
how truly
I've wounded my heart to get ahead, and still hear no reply but a gentle smile on your
face, and
a shake of your head.
You know, dear, how long and truly I've wounded my heart for goals, so don't tell the
world that
you're waiting for me.

Trademark

The miracle of being successful is having knowledge of your product, and working as a team.
People of all race are looking for the trademark, the president face to survive.
We are the young generation, the new face the world is facing, counting on our image and knowledge
to a better place. The trademark must continue its legacy from generation to generation, but can it?
Why must we fight? Knowing what we know at the end we're facing together. Yes! The answer we
think we know, not knowing God's plan is to bring his people to their knees.

We are the people of power and hope, we are the nation to a better waking – we are the hope,
the vision the slaves working to satisfy the trademark world we live in. We are the future. Common
air we share with the others, such as the mammals, the living sea of the underworld- compromising
our land, the wasted chemicals human kind stored to destroy the unfamiliar, the indifference we
cannot understand and the fight we tend to create.

It is in our nature to search for the trademark for security, it is our goal to put it to use in order to be profitable. Remember the good deed and the importance of our trademark and keep in
mind never to sell out to the refugee's who takes refuge in our country.

Unbreakable!

One door of happiness open and the other closes to waking us inside to a better place;
Many times we are looking at the one that is close that we forget to pay attention to
the one that is open to great opportunity.

Many people come and go in our lives like duck's flying south for the winter looking to take
a piece of me with them as far as memories they can hold on to. But only one true love have my
heart and so I speak of him freely and willingly.   "Unbreakable he is," favorable I am when I
hold him in the night whenever his vulnerable.
The smell, the touch, the feelings we shared are incredibly magical and unforgettable to let go,
Yes! It is said by strangers that the way we look together is so unbreakable that we combine as
one soul.

Love always bade him welcome, pain we endure every day 'cause of fear of being hurt', truly if
my heart can cry out only then I would go and bring him the moon, but until he shown be
differently perhaps I'll remain settled and unbreakable like a bonsai tree.
people talk the talk and not walk the walk, but with us we do lots more than just the talk the talk
we learn to Walk the walk and live by the rules.   "Unbreakable we are", incredible our love is for
one another. Its love like we learn to appreciate when asking sincerely to the higher power, Pain
and suffering escape us as we lay to complete silence. It's a matter of time that love came by.

About The Author

Growing up in the Island was hard for many middle class families in Haiti unless they inherited their parents Trust Fund. The Artist developed his skills at College Beard School for the gifted. It was then he discovered his passion for writing poetry. As an adult he began to search for answers but to find God as his witness and of course his poems for guidance. From the poetry that he has written over the years, he decided to share them by writing the book-title Époque meaning once upon a time in French.

www.ingramcontent.com/pod-product-compliance
Lightning Source LLC
Chambersburg PA
CBHW020406290526
45785CB00005B/2457